THE MYSTERY OF MISSING

ROHIT KUMAR DASH

Copyright © Rohit Kumar Dash
All Rights Reserved.

This book has been published with all efforts taken to make the material error-free after the consent of the author. However, the author and the publisher do not assume and hereby disclaim any liability to any party for any loss, damage, or disruption caused by errors or omissions, whether such errors or omissions result from negligence, accident, or any other cause.

While every effort has been made to avoid any mistake or omission, this publication is being sold on the condition and understanding that neither the author nor the publishers or printers would be liable in any manner to any person by reason of any mistake or omission in this publication or for any action taken or omitted to be taken or advice rendered or accepted on the basis of this work. For any defect in printing or binding the publishers will be liable only to replace the defective copy by another copy of this work then available.

To my loving wife

Jeetarani

And

My two most loving kids

Pritish And Prasim

Contents

1. Feedback — 1

2. War Or Peace — 3

3. A Way Away — 6

4. Poetry — 7

5. Crash — 8

6. Rain — 10

7. Quest — 11

8. The Tajmahal — 13

9. Teddy Bear — 15

10. My Teddy — 16

11. Writing — 18

12. Election — 19

13. Cruelty — 20

14. Betrayal — 21

15. You Are The Poem — 22

16. Vulgarity — 23

17. Rewrite Myself — 24

18. Hug — 26

19. Love Has No Religion — 28

20. Mystery — 30

21. Love — 31

22. The Uncertain World — 32

23. Birth Right — 35

24. The Path Of Truth — 36

Contents

25. Yet Untouched — 37

26. Simple Words — 39

27. The Mystery Of Missing — 41

28. Belief — 43

29. The Spring — 45

30. Arise Awake — 46

31. Spring — 47

32. Read Me — 48

33. Re-living — 50

34. Disappear — 52

35. The God — 53

36. The Open Door — 54

37. Destiny — 55

38. Love Bird — 56

39. Easy — 58

40. The Parting Words — 59

41. Black — 60

42. Poetry And Me — 61

43. Smart City — 63

44. The Story Of Self — 65

45. The Storm — 67

46. Money — 69

47. Special — 70

48. Bliss — 71

Contents

49. Innocence   72

50. God Is For All   73

51. To Become A Poet   74

52. Eligibility   76

53. War Time   78

54. Trust & Love   80

55. Level   82

56. Until How Long   84

57. Unique   86

58. Rain   88

59. At The End   89

60. The Last Song   90

1. Feedback

Oh creator!
You are really a
Wonderful creature
Tell me in your creation
Why there are
So many why
Why still then
You never feel shy
Why you still
Do not change your
Nature
Can you explain me
Why there are
Fury and fire
Hue and cry
I do not know but
Where to complain
Where to send our
Creative suggestions
You do not even have a
Complain box
For devotee's care
Like in banks

Or display your
Toll free number
To lodge our grievance
Is it fair ?

2. War or Peace

Peace peace peace

What we need is peace

Please do not cut the land

Piece by piece

The need of the hour

Is peace

But you never listen

Only think of thyself

You selfish.

You welcome war

Not peace

And now toiling in

Troubled water

Like a fish.

Oh ! no we do not need

A bomb to blast

Our's is a nation

Free of colour, creed or caste.

No more patience

No more tolerance

We can no more bear fury

Nor can bear even

A minor injury

Nor do we need a gun
Or any sharp weapon
To live on earth
For fear of war
The only thing we wish
Peace peace and peace.
Were we not born from the
Same womb
From mother earth
The same blood
Flowing in our vein
From our birth
We never thought our
Own brother will
One day turn our enemy
And will fight one day with us
For reason no any.
Is boundary ,boarder ,LoC
Everything.
Can't we cross the boarder
With a broader chest
And embrace each other
Can't we open up a little
Can't we move forward
With a lip full of smile
And a heart full of love
Can't we erase the

Boarder line
From the map
With an eraser
I think this will
Make things a
Little easier.

3. A way away

Let me live life

My way

Anybody desiring

To get rid of me

Let them be away.

Let me go

My way

Let me in my way

Go away.

Yeh! a way

Away

Other than

Anyone's way

Did you get me

Now

I am in a way

Most away

From a way

The real way

4. Poetry

The journey
of poetry
Is always
Towards
Eternity.
Let poetry
be a prayer
A prayer
for humanity.

5. Crash

Alas once again
My mobile has
been crashed
So many data lost
Many poems too
Which I was yet to
Share
Why it always
happens with me
Is it due to lack of care
Any way I am not to spare
But who cares
For the creative moment
I spent
Which may not
Come back to me
Again
The feelings
The emotions
Those were so rare
May I try again
But it too is in vain
A moment that is gone

Never comes back again

You should only have to learn

How to bear the pain

Now everything from

My mind has been washed

My mobile has been crashed.

6. Rain

Outside the train
It's only rain and rain
My heart cries in pain
I can't feel the shower
With barrier of this
Window pane
All efforts are
In vain
Let me adjust my
Feelings again
With the showering
Rain.

7. Quest

I may not be like other
But do not bother
Since my feelings
Are mine
And I am true to
My feelings rather.
How does it matter
You like me
Or dislike
Curse me
Or bless me
In disguise
I may not be able
To fulfill
All your dreams
And desire
May not be able
To meet all your
Expectations
Too do not believe
In self contentment
Nor wish to disappoint you
With any misconception.

But yet I am committed

Committed to a noble cause

Still on this voyage

I am in quest

Never claimed myself

The best

But surely can say

My work is novel

My feelings at least

Are not copy/paste.

8. The Tajmahal

I have read

Tajmahal was made

In memory of Mumtaz

By sahajahan a Raj

Who loved her truly

It was so expensive

Although so lovely

And is one among

The seven wonders

It was built by so many

Manson and workers.

In front of this great monument

I found you one day

Selling bangles

Although you look like

A beautiful nightingale

Your loved one lost her

Left leg one day here

For a slip on the marble

And now waits for you

For his bread in a

Cottage near the pine jungle.

You strive so hard

In this hard summer

Cold weather

In heavy rain

But never hesitate to

Throw a smile

For every passerby

Despite all your sorrows

sufferings and pain.

Now I could feel

Your love is better

Than that of Sahajahan

With all your love & sacrifice

For the dear one

You have yourself

Erected a great monument.

May be a Tajmahal ?

9. Teddy Bear

Hey ! dear
Can you here
Your love could
Make me nothing
Except a teddy bear
For you to play
In your sweet will and way
Not me
It is what they say.
Still I cheer
Dancing to your tune
Clapping with both
The hands
Like a teddy bear
With out any
Shame and fear
Can't you hear ?

10. My Teddy

My teddy
Is yet not ready
May be she is
Scared of her daddy
Let me not be so tidy
And write for her
A sweet melody
So that she can cheer
And I can present her
A teddy bear.
She is very smart
Tells teddy bear
Does not have a heart
But my dear
If to my teddy bear
You make even a slap
It will only dance and clap.
I think
This is the best thing
In today's stressful life
If you can laugh and be merry
In all your sorrows, sufferings and strife
My sweet lady

Can you find a gift better
Than what I decided to present
You here
For a happy life to marry for ever
And to live a joyful life
Filled with laughter
And unending cheer
With out tear and fear.

11. Writing

• 18 •

I am writing
And will be writing
Till my ink gets dry
I am helpless
If for that reason
Some one
Wants to weep and cry.

12. Election

Election is
The process
Of selection
In a democracy
By the people
Of the people
For the people.
But the irony is
The very word
Selection
Is now
Substituted
By corruption.
It has
Now become a
Profit making
Institution
Before and
After the
Nomination.

13. Cruelty

Cruelty !
Thy name is women
Said Shakespeare.
But what about
Their loyalty
In a homely
atmosphere .
By saying it
Cruelty
Feel you not guilty.

14. Betrayal

She betrayed me
I betrayed her
Time betrayed us
In the process
Of betrayal
One is always cruel
This is common
For one and all
So it is universal

15. You are the poem

Which is the
Poetry
You are
In search of
She told me once.
You are the
Piece of poem
I was in quest of
I told her at once
She left the room
By throwing a
Smile at me at a glance.

16. Vulgarity

It is said

Vulgarity

Always lies

In beholder's eyes

If I look vulgar

It is not me

This is what

Your eyes say

But you won't

Believe

The heresy

Still

Am I vulgar in

Anyway.

17. Rewrite myself

Getting a chance
I will rewrite myself
I could not live life
As I desired
Mostly I was so casual
So whimsical
And so on
My time expired.
No need to pant
Nothing to repent
It all depends
On the decision
you make
On that same moment
Life can not be
Lived as you want
At times
You are decided by them.
If ever I go back
And can work on it
I will make
All necessary
Correction

May be I could not
Make life of my choice
As per my projection.

• 25 •

18. Hug

Today I was feeling seek
For a tight hug
While early dawn felt
Suddenly embraced warmly
By someone from back
And found it was
No other by my dear pet dog
Who is far better any way
And never waits for a hug day.
Although a small dog
Offers and demands
Daily for a warm hug
But for whom I waited
For a hug for the whole life
They never turned up
They not only reacted
With ugly face
But alo pretended of having no time
Even when I found them
In a tight hug
Having no love
Full of some ill motif
Selfishness

They even did not spare to
Make myself wounded
Causing my tender heart
to ooz blood only
I felt like being in a hug
With a dagger or sharp knife
And I had to compromise with them
For my whole life.

19. Love has no religion

Love is neither Indian
Nor foreign
It is universal
And always reign
Love is the monarch and
Heart is its only domain.
Thus love has
No religion.
It is not based on
Caste color or creed
It too is not only made for the
Human breed
Birds animals insects
Serpentines and the whole cosmos
All are bound in this string
of love across
The world someday will
Sink in to oblivion
But love would still be
Shining in its horizon
There is no harm in love
So far it is gentle descent
Love is always so charming

With due proportion
Love has no set limit
Someday you may have to repent
If you neglect it.
In love I do not
Believe in a particular day
For me every day is a loving day
So with confidence I tell
Love is nothing geographical
It neither belong to
Any particular region
For love
There may be someday a big rebellion
So go on loving everyday
Atleast in small proportion
Let us love for the great humanity
For someday the world
May suffer due to lack of love
And collapse
Let us not just sit and relax
Love is only a word of charity
Let us not blame its sanctity
For the sake of love
If you want someone to crucify
Here I am ready for it
If I cold not justify.

20. Mystery

I stretched my
Both arm for a hug
But alas
It was all dark
Due to fog
I was so sorry
My hug has
Yet remained
A mystery.

21. Love

I lived my whole
Life
In search of love.
But it was such a
Difficult riddle
Which no one
could solve.

22. The Uncertain World

Nothing was certain
Even uncertainty
Itself was uncertain.
Nothing was secured
Even security
Itself was
Unsecured
Still all were lured.
There was a forecast even
That one day
All will suffer
And will be in the oblivion.
The soothsayers were
All busy making
Calculation
Many things were
Written on the forehead
Many a lines were
Drawn on the palm
Those were speaking of
The dark uncertain future
But all were so scared
But careless about tomorrow.

The dark day was approaching
All were locked down
In their premises
there were restrictions
To touch
To come in contact
To shake hand even
Was a curse
Masked faces
Were hiding the
Future
there was a chaos
Every where.
Even I could not
Recognize you
God as you were in mask
Even I could not
Recognize you
We behaved with each other
As if we were
Strangers
In front of us was a
Cursed world
Trembling seriously
With fear ,hate, enimity
Behaving so strange
Some were even busy

In revenge
For some making money
Was the game
Nothing could stop them
Nor fear of sin
Nor thought of innocent
Children
They went on playing
Their game
Knowing that
The world is
Temporary
Everything here
So uncertain
Here there is
No loss no gain
In a cyclic motion
You may turn to ashes
And may be here again.

23. Birth Right

Poetry
You never
Let me sleep
Nor let me
Write.
For you
I toiled whole night
Am I right
Despite
I never forget
And for you always fight.
Nor let you go
And followed you
Even in my dream
To set you right
I always hold you tight.
Admit you or not
Poetry
You are my
Birth right.

24. The Path of Truth

To pursue my dream
I chased truth
The path was
Too hard
To distract me
From my path
You followed me
As a bird.
After days of struggle
I am able to sing
But your voices
Yet to be heard.

25. Yet Untouched

I am always so busy
Catching you is
Not so easy.
You fly like a bird
Your voices
Often I heard
While I follow you
Like a bird
My wings get tired
Sometimes you appear
Sometimes disappear
Still I feel
You are always to me
So near and dear
Your sweet voice
I can still hear
Near my ear
At times I cant bear
When I feel
You are not near.
My life is dedicated
In your search
I have spent

My whole life

In your research.

But you have

Always remained

Untouched

Some day

I may lose my life

For you I am shocked.

26. Simple words

My words are so simple
And of course sober
I use them knowingly
To make your journey
To my world of poem smoother.
I want to say sometimes
Something very interesting
What the world need to know
But what if no one can hear me
If I speak slow.
I want to connect
To be connected with you
To listen to me
Are you not ready too.
Communication is
Always two way
Thus if I speak
My way
It must be ready
Too your way
So that we from each other
Can not be away.
Now listen to

What I say
May the world
Reacts its way
We must say our say
In a decent way.
Let us say thing better
The world is already
Suffering with all
Things bitter.

27. The Mystery of Missing

Never miss me
I am always in
My missing.
Only I seem to be missing
The fisherman never knows
Which fish to be caught
While fishing
I am always there
Where people think
I am missing.
May be in a troubled sea
In this great voyage
Of life
We are sailing
On the same boat
Not even being
sure about
Our destination
And destiny
May be that sense
of insecurity
Brings in us that illusion

No still I say I am not missing

No one ever misses

Even if they sincerely wish

In missing too

All are there

In their missing

No one is truly missing

If ever they miss

They miss in me truly

Again next moment

They are there

Where they were

And ought to be

In missing.

28. Belief

I died one day
With my life
As I don't know
How to live a
Pretentious life.
With so many
disharmony
Loneliness
Lifelessness
Without love
Compassion
Sympathy
apathy
I was really tired
And I decided to quit
As I was unable to adjust
Myself a little bit.
.

I am now living
A dead life
While other say
I am still alive anyway.
I can not go by others saying

As I still live a life
With what I really believe
And is living.

29. The Spring

I was half awake
While I was still asleep
You lured me to wake up
While I was tired enough
For a deep sleep.
You peeped through
The window of
My bed room
And called me
With my name
In your sweet voice
And declared
Your presence.
Yeah! it was as such
Possible to know
due to the fragrance
Of all the seasonal flowers
Those were in the wind
You still hold me tight
The sky was yet
Not bright.

30. Arise awake

All are walking
In their walk of life
After they wake up
In the hope of
Walking further.
But do they know
Either that
They are yet asleep
Yet to rise
Yet to wake up
And walk further
And further
And are yet
In a fake dream
Deeply drowned
In a sleep
And can't wake up even
With so many noises
So many scream.

31. Spring

If winter comes
Can spring be far
Behind
This idiom
Does not always
hold true.
If only you
Can find
Summer,winter ,spring
May be only a
State of mind.

32. Read me

Read me if you have time.
I may not be an open book
But always open for you
I find you always
In my heart
And do never feel apart
The door of my heart
Is always open
To where you can freely
Come and go
Now also in this
Darkness of night
Your memory
Haunts me.
I get nostalgic
Your love has
Always remained
So analgesic.
Now also in this
Starry sky
I see your dazzling eyes
In the silent breeze
I hear your voice sing untill you

complain me of love
That never seize.

33. Re-living

Getting a chance
I will rewrite myself
I could not live life
As per my choice
I could never rejoice
Mostly I was so casual
So whimsical
And so bychance
My time expired at once.
No need to pant
Nor to repent
It all depends
On the decision you take
On that particular moment
Life can not be lived
As you desire at times
You are decided by them.
If ever I go back
And can work on it
I will make all
Necessary correction
May be I could not
Make life

As per my projection.

34. Disappear

Oh God I was
So unmindful of you
While you came
But for that reason
Please do not blame.
For I do not find
Any more to mind
Whether you are aware of it
I still have a doubt
Despite sorry for not
Attending you
But you also left me
With out telling adieu

35. The God

I am a small ordinary man
But being a great God
Omnipresent
Why you can't be blamed
You always disappear
When you have to appear
Ghost or God still I fear
due to your disappearance
Despite people believe
One day you will
Change the whole world
The whole atmosphere
With your unusual
Behavior
even if you are not seen
to ordinary eyes
And always disappear

36. The open door

It all depends
On how you peruse things
Or how much you are
Awakened
Light pierce in
Even if you close
One door
The other is opened

37. Destiny

Despite all my trial
I am unable to
Come out of my problem
Oh God!
Why you always
Make a trial with
My destiny
I try, struggle
With all force
wth vigour and vitality
But trouble are always
By my side
You close your eyes
While I pray
As if I am destined to srife

38. Love Bird

A lone bird
My sympathy.
My warmth
For my love
My pity
My love
Welcome.
Next the fire
The scare
The desire.
No hurt
No harm
Come
Welcome.
Flew thee away
My eyes
My heart
Fixed
My love
With hunger
Mixed.
I stand
And wait

Wait and paint

You no come

Sweet bird

Always welcome.

39. Easy

Forgetting someone
Made easy.
Get yourself
Extremely busy.

40. The Parting Words

Leaving you all
With a heavy heart
Poetry
I never thought
Time will
One day
Keep me
Apart
Time you played
Too smart
But I know
You will ever be
In my heart.

41. Black

It is not necessary
That hairs should
Always be black.
And if I tell this
Some one may smack.
Let us not depend
Let us not pretend.
Let us face that
Let us accept this
Small fact.
May your goodly
Figure
Look distorted.

42. POETRY AND ME

Please do not
Take away poetry
From me
I can't live
A moment
Without her
I am alive
Till poetry
Is with me so far.
Poetry is my blood
That circulates in my vein
If it stops flowing
How some one can
Live again.
Poetry is my breath
That I respire
In to my lung
How can I live
Than with out
A song.
Poetry is the food
Which kept
Me alive

My hunger for poem

Made me to live.

Poetry is the water

Which drench my thirst

Poetry is my

Bread and butter

Which I add to my

Daily breakfast.

Poetry is the soul

Which lives

In my heart

Its vibration has

Always made me

Live a life so smart.

43. Smart city

Smart city
Searching for a smart man
Wait he is coming
To relieve you from
All your miseries and pain
Wait with patience till then.
May be this time
He may not sing a song
But will certainly
Assure you of moon and sun
With singing bird and dancing trees
With a sky full of stars
An evening scented with
Jasmine flowers
And a blue sea
With roaring waves
A sea beach with
Gentle breeze.
Putting his hand
On your shoulder
Will chant a poem rather
A song so sweet and smoother
Will have a promise to

Walk on the smart road
With your hand together.
Bhubaneswar a smart city
Full of joy and love
An intimate friend
Now the relationship
May will be stronger
With a magical bond.
Heart always thrives
To see you again and again
For which someone has
Already boarded the train.
With loads of
Old memories
Heavy on heart
With a heave of sigh
And love filled heart
And ofcourse
With a promise to
See you always
Again and again.

44. The Story of Self

The moment I
lost myself
Is the moment
I am myself
And the moment
I am with me
Is the moment
I am not myself.
And I am not with me
When I am with me
And when I am with me
I am not me.
Are you me
Or me myself
I am in you
You are in myself.
May be you too
Are myself
Me yourself
There are moments too
When no one is
No self.
A moment with zero self

Oh ! Let us get rid of

This horrible me

But its always with thee

An invisible ghost

A shade

A self

May it be me

Myself

Thyself

Self.

45. The Storm

Storm everywhere
Both inside and outside
Weather so crazy
Half eaten moon
Disappearing
Inside the black cloud
Gradually
Life was never full.
Unsettled dust and leaves
Waste paper of
A marriage feast
All making round
In this whirlwind
In the ground.
Where is the mind
Where?
Rain will come
The cloud is with
That promise
Storm may lose
ground with that
And will lose strength
But what about

The storm

That whirl inside

But who will

Relieve this

Inside pain.

46. Money

Money money
Money
Sweeter than honey
Does it not
At times
Seems very funny.

47. Special

May be big or small
I have problem with all
Not me
It is you who call
So why do not
You think
I am someone special
And me not like
Anyone at all.

48. Bliss

If you ignore me
I have to ignore you all
As relationship
Is always reciprocal
It is not as you wish
And mind you
Ignorance is
Not always a bliss.

49. Innocence

I sense the

Love sense

In all your

Sweet nonsense

May God

Keep alive

The child in you

And the child like

Innocence.

50. God is for all

Red yellow white or purple
Does not matter how big or small
May be on temple may be on wall
May be laying
On street for sell
May be a piece of stone
With no shape at all
May be rich
May be poor
May be costly
Or may be dear
May be without a pie at all
Big or small
God is for all.

51. To Become a Poet

It is not necessary
To write a poem
To become a poet
Not it is required for a
Poet to write a poem.
My be you have to
Live a poem
To be a poet
Or someone living
A poem is a poet.
You become a poet
Even if you do not
Utter a single word
But you only see and
Perceive things
You react but not
Like others
You can not only be a
Silent spectator.
You see the silent bird
Slowly flying on to the sky
You see a flower blossoms
And a butterfly moving

Around it
you see a distance mountain
Standing patiently
You see a calm river murmuring
You see a sea roaring.
But everyone
Who see them does not
Become a poet
Nor it is mandatory
To become a poet
To see all these
Despite one is a poet
may be some arer born poet
some are made poet
and on some as shakespeare said
becoming poet is
Thrust upon them.

52. Eligibility

Some are more eligible
Than other
You are more eligible
From someone
Still they rule
Although they are
Less qualified than you
They are in a higher
Position
And you have to
Obey simply their rule.
People still complain
Of this gross inequality
You strive to bring parity
And lose yourself
In charity
They know about
Your eligibility
But cant't see the vanity
Although it is still day
And there is clear visibility.
In an unequal world
It is possible

The weak poses stronger
The fool wiser
And they find you
Always ineligible.

53. War time

It was war time.
I told them
It is no time
To write a poem
Sitting relaxed
At home
It is time you set for war
With gun and grenade in hand.
The whole world is
Under bomb
So many corpse
No ground for tomb
Nor even tear
In our eyes to weep
All are exhausted
To console for
Wound so deep.
Still you request me
To write a poem
Sorry I have
No time for them.
If you still force me
To write a poem

Let me sing a song
To inspire them
War is not the last
Resort
Let us come ,sit together
And have a dialogue
For our comfort
Let us do not confront
Let us not grunt
Let us bring peace
In our forefront.

54. Trust & love

The world is now
Suffering from
Lifelessness
There is lack of love
Lack of trust
Lack of peace
The world is now
Cut piece by piece.
Their is no mutual
Understanding
No harmony
Thus the world is
Divided in to segment
We are just a small
Fragment.
What happened to
This beautiful world
Was it due to selfishness
Was it due to lack of love
Lack of trust
Mutual harmony.
Who spoiled this world
Here we sipped nectar

Who mixed poison in it
Now it is time to think
Now let us all think
For a moment
How to save this beautiful world
From a debacle
As soon devoid of love
The world will sink
Before that
Let us somewhere sit
And think.

55. Level

There are different levels
You have to find yours.
You don't find a
Perfect match
And cant accept what
ever you fetch
Hence there is
Always a mismatch.
All are not your level
But still then with them
You have to travel
They may even for
No reason grumble
It is in their preamble
And may even quarrel
But for that reason
You do not have to
Postpone your travel.
You see you are
Already boarded the flight
With a valid ticket
To travel is now your right.
Can you stop the flight

In the midway
You are now in air
To think to cancel
The jouney is not
Possible
Nor even fair
But you have to cry
In despair.
You are shipwrecked
In a troubled sea
Now everywhere
There is water and water
To accept the truth
And fight for the
Situation is still better.
You should have planned
The journey before the travel
Your life now depends
Much on the sea
And the sea level.

56. Until How Long

There is no solution
For this endless pollution.
We are grasping for breath
For pure air
The leaves of the trees are
Covered with dust
Even trees are rare
There is forest
But not at their best
We sacrificed them
For industrialization
In the name of civilization.
The rivers have dried
The clouds have no rain
Birds and animals are
In real pain
As everything is misused
By men
The birds die
Due to the mobile tower
The sun does not have
The strength
To make bloom a flower

For the vibration

For the radiation

We lost in nature

Our most beautiful Creature

Still we hold seminar

In the name of protecting

Environment

In big hotels in Ac rooms

In the name of seminar

Glorifying nature

We sing beautiful song

But we are still cheating ourselves

And do not know untill how long.

57. Unique

All are unique
Their own way
As they say
All may not be the same
None to blame.
Let a single moon bloom
And under it
Thousand flower blossom.
They are all part of this
Beautiful creation
No harm if they have
Their own notion
Not that all flower will
Bear the same fragrance
Of rose, jasmine or lavender
For that may be they are not borne
Not that all flower will be as
Beautiful as
Lotus,Marigold or daffodil
Think a little.
Let us say
Everybody has an unique
role to play

May everybody sing
Their own song
I don't find there is
Anything wrong.

58. Rain

I love rain

So also you

But my love

For rain

Can never

Be compared

With you

It is unbelievable

but true.

59. At The End

Let me begin
At the end
That nothing really ends
In the cyclic motion of life
we are back again
From where we started
So let us not calculate
In miles
Let us not in this journey
Feel exhausted
Still we have hope
And we must hope for
better things
And like Eliot let me say
In the end is my beginning.

60. The last song

This may be my last song
Who knows
Who has seen tomorrow
Yes I do not beleive
In those predictions
That tomorrow such and such
Things may happen
I do not beleive in those
Jodiac sign
Not in the lines on
Fore head and palm
I am still calm
And can say this is no wrong
If Icall this my last song.